GW00602773

TIANO

Covering Columbus

Edited by Abdul Malik

Poems and Stories Marking 500 Years of Caribbean Unsettlement

Published by **Panrun Collective 1992**

Financially assisted by The Arts Council

Copyright © Panrun Collective 1992

All rights reserved

Cover design by Kamal Singh Matthews

Cover: Batik & Acrylic Painting -
Touchau - the Storyteller by Kamal Singh Matthews

Typeset by Creole Books

Printed by RAP Ltd. 201 Spotland Road,
Rochdale OL12 7AF

ISBN 0 9513173 2 6

Panrun Collective exists to promote the work of
Caribbean artists (poets, performers of poetry and other
creative writers) through publishing, recording, teaching,
lecturing and organising performances and workshops.

Panrun Collective
46A Trent Road
Brixton
London SW2 5BL
Tel: 071 274 3292

For the children of the nineties

Aïdah, Yaasi, Ayesha and Latifah

Special thanks to Jenny, Mike, Foufou and the Collective for all their hard work.

Contents

Panrun Collective reproduces this statement by the SAIIC to augment the scope and purpose of this anthology. Near Wounded Knee, a poem by one of our members, bears testimony.

An Alternative to the Columbus Day Celebration

We, at the South and Meso-American Indian Information Centre (SAIIC) call on all people to join together in creating an alternative to the Columbus Day celebrations. This is a call to all people to reflect on what the last 500 years of colonization of the American continent has meant to you personally, to your people, to the people of this world, and to Mother Earth.

1992 will mark 500 years since the arrival of Columbus' genocidal forces on this continent. 12 October marks the so-called "Discovery", or no less misnamed "Encounter of Two Worlds". For Indian people of the Americas, this date marks the beginning of an invasion of the continent. This invasion took place with the explicit purpose of exploiting the natural resources of this continent to supply European elites with the least expensive resources possible. The invasion has been taking place for 500 years without the slightest regard for the Native people of this continent. We ask the Spanish government, the United States government, the Vatican, and all Latin American and European governments who are promoting the Quincentennial Jubilee, how the total steam-rolling of cultures for the enrichment of a European minority can be considered an "Encounter of Two Worlds"? We want the truth to be known by the people of the world. The myths about Columbus and the "Encounter" are a completely false manipulation of history.

The most evident consequences of the European invasion are genocide, torture, political, ideological and cultural submission and death through diseases brought to the continent. Our land and our resources have been, and continue to be, plundered. Military, ideologic, economic

1

and religious power are the instruments of domination in this conquest.

We are still witnessing colonial aggression today. The conquest of the Amazon is a very clear example of this. This land is under assault in order to exploit its mineral resources, its reserves of valuable timber and hydro-electric potential. The Indian people of the Amazon are confronting this conquest, and this is 1991! The Yanomami, the most populous of the indigenous people of the Amazonian rainforest, are facing the loss of their lands and are being killed because they are viewed as a barrier to the maximum exploitation of natural resources in Brazil. When Indian people in El Salvador or Guatemala work their traditional lands communally to feed their families, and this interferes with the provision of cheap natural resources to the "developed world", they are slaughtered. The Canadian army invades the Kahnawake Mohawk Reservation when the Mohawk people attempt to protect traditional lands from the expansion of a golf course! The truth is that the atrocities of the early years of the European invasion continue unabated today. We realize that we are just one population of many which have been and continue to be victimized by the system imposed upon us by the Western/European culture. African-Americans, brought to this continent as slaves and the Mestizo populations continue with us in our struggles for freedom, justice and respect.

We are calling on all sectors of society to form an alliance to counter the planned Quincentennial Jubilee and demand that governments, religious and educational institutions tell the truth about what took place 500 years ago and examine how these injustices continue today.

On 17-21 July 1990, nearly 400 Indian people, representing 120 nations, tribes and organizations of the Western Hemisphere met for the first time in Quito, Ecuador, to discuss their peoples' struggles for self-determination and strategize for a unified Indian response to the 1992 Jubilee celebrations. Despite the offensive denial of truth in the official histories, we choose instead to use this symbolic date to reflect upon what the invasion meant to us, to work with a renewed effort for our autonomy, to educate the people of the world, to celebrate that we are still here and our cultures are still alive thanks to 500 years of resisting, and to formulate alternatives for a better life, in harmony with Mother Earth. We at SAIIC are serving as a liaison between Indian people of the South and Indian people of the North, as well as educating the general public about what the past 500 years has meant to Indian people in South and Meso-America and how they are strategizing for change.

There exist many myths among Indian people from all over the Americas which say that this period of oppression will last for 500 years and we would enter a period of change (**Pachakutek**) and the oppression will end. We believe we are now in **Pachakutek**. Join us in support of native peoples in 1992 and beyond.

(POB 7550, Berkeley, CA 94707, USA)

Near Wounded Knee

The tatooed Sioux
(blue prison numbers up his left forearm)
shows me two stone arrowheads
(his heritage)

.

"Know what these are?" he asks

.

Pleased with me for answering right
he offers a ride to Rapid City
in his beaten-up Oldsmobile
(and I'd set out to walk to the top of the ridge)

.

"So you're from England,"
says his long-haired, reservation-softened friend
who sits in front rolling a leafy cigarette

.

"How do you like **our** country"

?

The driver seems to like my answers;
he offers me the bottle he's been swigging from
and accelerates up the dusty trail

.

But we aren't on the road I want
and I'm relieved
when they let me off at the next fork

.

The early morning sun is already cooking the Dakota air
so I risk the rattlesnakes and hurry
through the Badlands back to camp

.

I don't have the stomach for trading-post whisky
before breakfast

.

Mike Cleary

4

Tiano...

a title ... an entitlement ... a monuMENTAL effort to
highlight Amerindian displacement ... TIANO ... a
word-sound ... a meaning ... gracious ... sonorous ...
strenuously invoked ... TIANO-O-O-O ... the lost
word-chord intoning the loss ... intoning the lost meaning
... intoning the present ... intoning ... intoning ... the
present dearth of history ... TIANO ... a concerted portrayal
of the depths of Caribbean unsettlement ... the heights of
Caribbean resolve ... TIANO ... placing the displacement ...
linking ... the meaning ... passing ... the word-play ... on
... to Shake Keane's accompanying note ... key note poem
"People Like We" first sounded at the first Carifesta -
Guyana 1972 ... Shake ... with the spirit ... says,

"The alternative title of this poem is **Nation Shout**. The
poem is a celebration of Ethnic Responsibility. Let
Columbus "discover" whatever he discovered ...
This poem is about collaboration between at least two of
Our People, represented by their ancient gods:-
Makonaima and Qualeva. The collaboration extends, and
embraces us all."

TIANO-O-O-O ... a word-sound ... enchanting ... a
word-chord ... enhancing ... TIANO ... an Arawak word
meaning ... PEACE ... we give thanks ...

Abdul Malik

5

THE NEW GENESIS

Nation Shout

Makonaima say:
  touch me finger
  and let today
  be the day
  when all mountain
  lock they finger
  in the midst of the sea

Qualeva say:
  yes

Wind say:
  touch me throat
  and let today
  be the day
  to thread all voice
  through all valley
  and let there be
  in the midst of all music
  one note

Drum say:
  yes

Flute rattle and sitar
stand up like lip
            and breast
            and finger
            making
one mountain
            dreaming
one star
            locking
one love
            in the midst of the sea

People like we say:
  yes

Shake Keane

9

ANTI-GENESIS

(I)

Hell's Midden Kitchen

OUR FATHER...all seeing being giving Spirit AIOMON KONDI, wander through our world all the Spirits of the brown skinned people lived up high in the mountains and they would at times come down to Earth Mother, beating shaman drums, blowing on wind flute or dancing the sacred dream of creational power.

IT was the year 1492. The oracle stones foretold of the coming of pain and suffering, rivers of blood, trees, plants, fish, and four legged things, two legged things and all living beings...would NEVER be the same, it was as if the heavens opened and the earth span at a faster speed .... But still we ARAWAKS welcomed them, like brothers... some of us did not. They had men of learning ... We taught them about the WORLD, the MOON, the SUN, and the MEANING OF LIFE.

They told us about Guns, Swords, Killing, Sex...and Profanities. We gave them their pleasure..!

Like Animals they ravaged on the breast of our women. They gave us Smallpox, Measles, Common Cold, Drink, Death, Stress, Cities, Confusion, DEATH, Christianity, Civilization,
DEATH... AIDS... DEATH... DEATH.

WE gave them,
Papaya, Passion Fruit, Pineapple, Cashew Nut, Brazil Nut, Kidney Bean, Sunflower Seed, Guava, Butter Bean, Cocoa, Scarlet Runner Bean, Marrow, Maple Sugar, Capsicum, Sweet Corn, Plantain, Sweet Pepper, Sweet Potato, Cassava, Jerusalem Artichoke, Vanilla, Potato, Peanut, Avocado Pear, Banana, Yam, Herbs, Spices, Tomato, Aubergine, Peyote, Jimson Weed, Mushroom-Humito, and the Sacred spiritual Tobacco Herb, etc, etc, etc....

When we were giving,
they said it was for the better of all Mankind.
When they came for medical research we gave them

Plants, Barks, Fungi, Hard Wood, Soft Wood.
We taught them Mineralogy, Gold, Silver, Bauxite, Copper, Diamonds,
Oil, Coal, Water, Aluminium, Crystals, Quartz, Granite, Mica, etc...
We gave them animals, birds, fish, microbes and we the Living Microcosms.
From their Findings......their Surviving... 1+?=£££$$$..,
and we Amerindian Amazonian Native American Indians slowly Die from Servitude and Germ-War-Fare.
They said it was for the better of all Mankind,
but we have learnt that they are a ... kind of man
and we are.....HUMAN-BEINGS.
When their Missionaries came speaking of Universal Love
Christ Child and the Beginning..
We said.....YES...YESssss...We too have a Beginning.??

From the hole in the sky
From our Astral Dreaming
From our Carnated lives...We have a Beginning
The great Spirit all Seeing, Giving, Loving, Caring,
Aiomon Kondi, Arawidi, Tamosikabotano, Kamonatu, Makonaima
and the coming of Amalivaca man-child of Wind and Rainbow
Prophet of human-beings, Son of light
When Amalivaca Canoe runs to shore
We sing Praises of his return.

"Amalivaca, Amalivaca.....Amalivaca
inventor of the Woilbaka
Amalivaca, Amalivaca.....Amalivaca
Builder of Benabs
Amalivaca, Amalivaca..... Amalivaca
Child of the Wind and the Rainbow
Child of the Wind and the Rainbow
Child of the Wind and the RainbowwwwWWWWwwww".

When they told us about this Universal Christ child,
We said..."YES...YES...go see our bisiri and tell him".

14

When they came to me I learnt their language, and Read
their Books, the Oracle...forewarned...the silk cotton
tree
Lightning Eel, Thunder Axe, Mystic secrets of the Great
Spirits
Foretold of these beings from across the sea,
some came for peace..!
But there were thousands, billions who came for more
EL Dorado and the Cities of GOLD
EL Dorado and the City of £$%£+?=!!!

I hear they have a city called the big apple
Disney land, and other illusions of grandeur
more technology for the demons of wizardry
eating up the land
eating up the land
Till we shall be no more
just like the dodo

just.. like.. the .. dodo.

But still we have Eagle Heart, Amadlozi AmaZulu
and the spiritual war goes on

signed: Haburi c/o Tuup Hell's Midden Kitchen

Arawak Adventurer

1

Nature creates, nature liberates;
Plunging through earth-shaking greenery,
Feeling the pulse rise
To a point of no return;
Nature hurts, nature heals,
Life beyond death,
Rain-drop face beyond sweat.
Tracking the deer and wild-cat,
Exploring the pool of the giant cray-fish,

Assured by the action of bow and arrow;
Nature destroys, nature reveals
The secret foam of the sea-monster's splash,
The splash against a rock,
Rock, teeth-stained, blood-drained steel veins.

2

Instinct moving across the land;
Sparkling, invigorating rover
Riding a dolphin, chanting,
Translating the lobster's song.
Iron-hand, stone-shield,
Proud head held high,
Injected beyond visibility;
Sharp muscle strikes,
Separates the roaring ocean, and slays
The cunning sperm whale.

3

Odysseus dives through the tension
Of the cracked sky,
Stands on a holy pyramid
Hidden in a cluster of olive-trees
And trumpets his bravery:
'I AM THE WAY, THE TRUTH AND THE LIGHT ',
And the thunder broke
In acquiescence with the persuasive voice.
The hero captures the sweetness of every season,
His vision crawls between
Superstition and survival.

4

Man is a hunter.
The magic of his skill
Traps the agility of the tiger,
And in wild pageantry
Enhances his insatiated ego;
Stone-hammer, bone-knife
Conquer and penetrate the stormy islands.

Faustin Charles

Aximu`s Awakening

This morning the sun
tickled my eyes
as usual

and I slid from
my hammock
and looked at the skies
as usual

I yawned and I stretched
I felt like a splash
in the cold morning water
so I made a dash
towards the path
to the sea
before Ama could call me
and give me a work.

As I burst through the bush
at the top of the hill
I froze and I shivered
my heart stood still

Great canoes with houses
and clouds of cloth wings
hung on poles, full of wind,
strange frightening things
on the sea!

"Great Iocuhuuague Maorocon"
I whispered and knew
those terrible canoes
were coming for me.

Pamela C. Mordecai

The Curse of Terawak

(extract from a story)

An old Arawak legend tells that it was the curse of a Great Prophet Chief called Terawak, who ruled over the Arawaks in South America, that changed the island of Jamaica from the idyllic country it was to what it is today.

According to the legend this change took place long after the Arawaks came to the island, and just before the first Europeans arrived in 1494.

The legend says that Terawak had a dream one night in which the Great Spirit who lived in the sky urged him to leave with his people in long canoes for an island in the blue sea which he would reveal to them. They were to take only their wives and children as all their needs would be met in this new land. The Great Spirit had even named this new land. He told him that the name was an apt description and that they would instantly recognize it when they saw it. The Great Spirit also told him what would eventually befall this land. But Terawak, who was an old man, felt that his people would be better served in this great undertaking by a younger man in the leadership position, so he chose a young chief, Jaffetawak, to lead them.

For a long time the new leader and the people prepared themselves for their epic journey under the direction of Terawak. Great long canoes were made from giant cottonwood trees. Deer and other wild animals were hunted and killed in numbers as never before, their flesh roasted and turned into pemmican. The Arawaks prepared for their journey with unsurpassed inspiration. For they were glad to leave their South American homeland, glad to escape the onslaughts of the more warlike Amerindian tribes - the Aztecs, Mayans, Caribs, especially the Caribs. It was the latter's never-ending raids of death and destruction which had indeed prompted their departure. Deliverance had come. The great hand of providence had safely guided them across the great water as at long last their eyes beheld XAMACA - LAND OF SPRINGS.

The legend says that the entire island was then like a vast tropical garden, with many rivers, ponds, and springs teeming with turtles and a wide variety of fish. Gently undulating hills, not the craggy hill tops and high mountain peaks, nor the sheer valleys, caves and ravines so evident today, but verdant plains and fern-covered valleys. Thick evergreen vegetation covered the interior, natural haven to a rich variety of small animals and exotic birds of every hue and kind. Fruits and flowers grew in abundance filling the air with perfume so rare; mangoes, rich golden yellow, glowing in the sun, succulent, sweet as the sweetest sugar cane. Avocados, oranges, nazeberries, june plums, custard apples, bananas, cocoplums, guineps, to name some of the many fruits that grew wild in the forests. The legend says that gold, now hidden from view, littered the ground like common stones, adorning the mouths and beds of small streams and slow running rivers. So commonplace was gold that only the best high grade pieces were ever utilized in intricate designs for the bodies of the beautiful Arawak women. And they were thankful to the Great Spirit for bestowing upon them such bountiful gifts.

Now safe from the onslaughts of their unfriendly neighbours, they soon grew in numbers throughout the length and breadth of the country. Saved from the terror of war, the peace-loving Arawaks organized themselves in the most civilised manner. Murder, rape, stealing and violent disputes were unknown; individual honesty, respect and collective consideration for the welfare of all was the order of the day. They developed neither fighting skills nor implements of war, but actively sought individual distinction in developing and displaying skills integrated with the sustenance and enhancement of life.

Around settlements throughout the country were the neatest of gardens cultivated with every known kind of ground provision: yams, cassavas, cocas, dasheens, tanyas and accams, corn, peas, pumpkins, melons, and the inevitable sweet potato. The sweet potato was everywhere. Mauve, pink, yellow, some as large as the largest pumpkins seen in the markets of today. This was the vegetable most used in their celebrations, especially at the major festival - the harvest of sea and land - when all the people congregated.

Around the coastline, the most beautiful and serene scene graced the eyes. Coconut palm trees laden with nuts, their spreading fronds slow moving, caressed by gentle trade winds as soft as a maiden's breath. Far out on the horizon, sea and sky blended into softest blue reflecting balmy days and nights in fairest XAMACA.

The legend says that what is now known as Discovery Bay, marking the coming of Columbus, was the very place where the Arawaks commemorated their own arrival. It was here in this lovely cove, located on the northern coast, that their forefathers and mothers had landed. It was here they celebrated the harvest of sea and land; here they marked each end and new beginning of their cycles of life with prayers to the Great Spirit, the provider of the cooling breeze and soothing rain, the provider of the sacred fish and beautiful women for the men to take as wives. Yes, it was here on this sacred ground that the Arawaks congregated in their numbers to commemorate their arrival in XAMACA, LAND OF SPRINGS, with a variety of activities lasting several days and nights. Activities highlighted by canoe racing, swimming, fishing and storytelling contests, sweet potato tasting, the giving and receiving of gifts, electing new leaders and consecrating marriages. The harvest of sea and land was especially stimulating to the bodies and minds of these peace-loving and gentle people. Especially stimulating as story-tellers representing different clans vied with each other. One can imagine the rapt attention, the intensity of efforts, as stories recalling their epic journey to XAMACA were told and retold. One can imagine the transformation, especially at nights, of this lovely cove into a living, pulsating shrine, as torches blazed from a thousand canoes dancing on the sea floor. One can imagine the breathless pauses, the shouts and the cheering which accompanied the highly skilled acts of night-time spearing of the fish.

According to the legend, it was in the closing stages of one particularly successful and enjoyable harvest that the customary relating of Terawak's prophecy was to stamp itself in the minds of the Arawaks forever.

The legend says that Casawak, overall ruler of the Arawaks of XAMACA, was highly venerated and that he had ruled with the people's consent far longer than any other chief in living memory. His reign and stature were as long and influential as that of the Great Prophet, Chief Terawak. Though he was very advanced in age, he had nevertheless performed all of his duties at this particular harvest with his customary confidence and dignity. As grand master of ceremonies and spiritual leader of the nation, it was his awesome responsibility to initiate, preside over, conclude and usher in every new cycle with the blessings of the Great Spirit.

The blowing of conch shells and stamping of feet now greeted his appearance, bedecked in the most symbolic regalia. Around his neck, a replica of the blue marlin, their sacred fish; around his head, a wreath made of palm leaves, sweet potato vines, and an assortment of flowers. The legend says that Casawak began his address when there was complete silence, so that none of his words would be lost to any ear....

Then, only the humming bumble bee,
The busy banana bird
And the gentle, dashing, splashing sea
Would dare their voice make heard.

But it soon became obvious to everyone that his words were being delivered with great difficulty, and worse yet, tears were welling in the depths of his eyes. Closing them, he said :
"Our Great Father Terawak told us of the evil that would befall this land. It will take place not many moons after I go to the Great Spirit."

A great moan greeted these words, and Casawak, now shaking visibly like a branch of a tree in the grip of some unseen hand, began speaking in a voice such as they had never heard before:
"From these hills around us will come, as a result of a great trembling of the Earth, high mountains with craggy peaks, deep ravines and dark caves. Iguanas and lizards, so timid

21

and so tame, will change into ferocious alligators and crocodiles. Blood sucking bats and mosquitoes will cover our land. The sweet water we drink from our ponds and springs we will have no more. Out of them will come swamps and morass, and, out of these, will come the plague killing many of us."

Lifting his quivering arms above his head in supplication to the Great Spirit, he told his people that they should never forget to live for each other as the times ahead would be terrible:
"Many new Caribs will come and take our land. These new Caribs will be unlike those our fathers knew. The new Caribs will have bows without strings, and arrows our eyes will not see as they fly through the air."

The legend says that Casawak clearly saw the end of his people's life of contentment - destroyed by these "new Caribs".

But when the vibrating throughout his body had subsided and his eyes looked out on them once more, he spoke with the voice of comforting assurance that they knew. He told them the Great Spirit had promised them a far happier life: their gentle spirits would ever be able to roam in their land of springs, ever free to explore and admire its hidden beauty forever and ever.

No trace of any Arawak settlement or village remains in Jamaica today. These civilised, peaceful, defenceless but proud people left behind just a few artefacts and cave paintings in Cudjoe Hill, St. Catherine. They perished in those caves in which they sought refuge from the "new Caribs".

Yet today, from every village, town and hamlet come reports of mysterious sightings at nights of a strange, unknown people snaring birds and spearing fish. Yes, they still roam their beloved XAMACA, these people of a bygone age, although most times unseen....

Hymie Wilson

Lament of an Arawak Child

Once I played with the hummingbirds
and sang songs to the sea
I told my secrets to the waves
and they told theirs to me.

Now there are no more hummingbirds
the sea songs are all sad
for strange men came and took this land
and they are very bad.

They made my people into slaves
they worked them to the bone
they beat them and they wore them out
now there are almost none...

Today we'll take a long canoe
and set sail on the sea
we'll steer our journey by the stars
and find a new country.

Pamela C. Mordecai

A People Gone

I see you much more keenly now, first Jamaicans,
in your Xaymaca, your land of wood and water
in your early Caribbean sun and sea and winds.
I take this coastal walk from the Priestmans River
to Long Bay and feel a place breath soaked
and tracks-trampled by you, Arawak Indians,
without donkeys or cattle or wheels or a gun.

Roofs cone-shaped, your round houses of straw
make a village, isolated or sprawling on,
drummed by rolling of the sea and sung to
by the squawks of macaws and parrots.

And in the chatter on the seasound light,
helper children too colour-streak the day
while nearly naked men dig into the bulk
of a fallen silk cotton tree with instruments
of stone, wood and bone to find
a canoe there in the trunk oversized.

At another house other men make traps for fish
as they could have been tricky crosses of wood
with a noose to hold wild hogs, iguanas, birds.
At another house, other men and women make
ornaments, cloths, hammocks, instruments.

Further away, bordered by flame trees, guava,
starapple, away from the ordered crops
of cassava, maize, arrowroot, sweet potatoes,
and the bitter broad leaves of robust tobacco,
the backs bent as if on all-fours are women
sowing well soaked grain into fresh land.

And noises of excitement lead me. I stand
in a clearing of wood
seeing batos, your ball game, played.

On smooth stones arranged, spectators sit.
Centrally on carved stools
the caciques are together.
Eyes follow the ball, hit by shoulders or head
to receive explosions of praises
mixed with groans and wailful contempt.

From the tracks that lead me now, I see
at every house, the mane of black hair treated,
dressed. I see the light brown skin of wide
noses and broad faces getting specially painted.
A travel of cooking and brewing embraces me.
A festival! A festival dictates
the clusters of doings. The building
of a festival is the collecting of extravagance.

I stand, where all happens, the place of the man
who receives the best of sea and land harvests,
man who alone when in the trauma of death
will be honour-strangled for his release. I am
at the grounds of the cacique's house.
From everywhere, one people have come.

Striped and painted flat in red,
yellow, black, many men are also
feather cloaked and feather head-dressed.

In sounds of leg rattlers and other shell
ornaments, in chants of cries and groans,
good spirits are honoured against bad ones.
In all his painted and plumed glory and pendants
of carved amulets and bone and shell adornments,
the cacique heads the parade around the village
beating a wooden gong. Priests, at the rear,
and medicinemen, follow singing songs
that their voices alone will not defile.
Back to the grounds of the cacique's house
it is the time for the feasting and drinking,
the wild singing and dancing, and smoking.

And like returning from fishing
your canoes come in from other places
and from other parts of your island.
Like birds know their flight tracks
you know your way on the sea.
Yet, like an unknown is threatening
your song of prophecy tells
of behind-the-horizon strangers
who one day would arrive, with bodies covered
and armed with a thunder and a lightning.

Truly, one day, ploughing the high seas
with maps and guiding instruments
and a steady eye on a star,
travelling by God and guessing
well heightened with dreams of gold and spices,
of expansion and wealth and power,

Columbus and men arrived
on your island of Xaymaca.

Terror turned to goodwill.
These new people must be gods!
You brought gifts to Columbus.
You sought exchanges.
You sought new knowing Columbus brought.
Was it true, that attracted to Columbus' sword
you grasped it and blooded yourself?
Were these new looking people gods? Were they?
Carrying a Spanish official across a river
you dropped him in,
you held him down,
he drowned.
You stayed, you waited, you watched:
you tested and saw he really rotted.

And in the new tone and rhythm of voice
you were harrassed for gold.
You were made target practice
and dropped from fatal blows.
Made victims of small pox and other diseases
you died everywhere.
Made a slave labourer
you dislocated your being.
And O mismeasured, discounted, distressed,
swamped by demands for your
days, nights, your land,
you poisoned yourselves in groups
you hung yourselves in company
you dressed up your families and drowned yourselves.
And O Arawak people
in some short decades all of you were gone.

I sit now on the edge of a cliff.
I look out and over sunlit waves, remembering
the sea as your farm and big way of travel.
Remembering, bones of a whole people
the sea rocked and the earth reversed.
Remembering, my African footprints overlay
yours that the earth erased.

Remembering, the selfstyled 'masters' pour out
no elegies for you.
For memory's sake
I give you all of this, my little eloquence.

James Berry

Old Indian, Remembering

The history books were right
about one thing,
we did die, numerically,
like flies.
What they didn't mention
was the mumbled way we cursed ourselves,
even as the cord of death tightened
around our breath,
we cursed ourselves, more than we cursed them,
for the "Tiano" that came so ready to our lips.
And how we still yearn
after all this time to fight it out
in the green arena of the jungle,
skin grating skin, like iguanas,
without the quaking cowardice of the gun.

Grace Nichols

Taino Peace (A Dub Prayer)

Arawaks was
di first set a backs
dem man climb on
was the first set
a forehead
dem burst with gun
was the first set

a woman dem
weigh down pon

God
that conjunction
that declension
fornication
degradation
wicked genocidal
dread deadly
grievous hot bled
blood evil
flood of foreign
folly cruel
criss cross
whiteman dolly
zipping through
a generation
decimating
a whole nation -

What a cause
for celebration!

Arawaks was
di first set a backs
dem man climb on
was the first set
a forehead
dem burst with gun
was the first set
a woman dem
weigh down pon.

Dem ruinated
redman
dem rapinated
redwoman
deserve
little attention.
Who asking

that their red souls
rest in peace?
Who begging
that the quiet
of their culture
be released
once more
into these
Antilles?

Only idiot believe
that dead man tell
no tale...them
dead redman
dem raped redwoman
dem telling
rosaries of curses
wishing the worsest for these
once-their-home places
the traces
of that early plunder
stay with us
the gentle graces of
the Tainos will not
descend till we make
amends for their
destruction

till we anoint
with grief
with prayers
with lamentation
the annihilation
of their nation.

Arawaks was
di first set a backs
dem man climb on
was the first set
a forehead
dem burst with gun
was the first set

a woman dem
weigh down pon.

Required:
repentance
reparation
reverence
for this ruined nation

Rest them, oh Father,
in the peace
in which they living
were "discovered";
discover for us
Father living
in the violence
which found them
the lost Taino peace.

Arawaks was
di first set a backs
dem man climb on
was the first set
a forehead
dem burst with gun
was the first set
a woman dem
weigh down pon.

Grieve for this nation.

Rest their souls, Father,
rest them and release
the Taino peace.

Pamela C. Mordecai

ANTI-GENESIS

(II)

Ships of Columbus

It was like Dream-Vision
Many many different images
I see ... some good..
I see ... some bad..
I see ... some neither good or bad.
Only Makonaima and Orehu know. I see Big Long Boat,
Spirit Ship
Wading into the Harbour
Like an Asgardean Rainbow Myth
big big like I never seen before,
Well not in my time ... or my Father's Father's time, but
long,
Long, before then .. when people with skin like gold,
Dark purple blue and mud like red.... lived...
There's a story in that!
But that was my father's time..... and I will tell you of mine.

"What year was this?" you ask. 1492 ... I will not forget the
Long
Boat with woven hammocks stretched out to dry.
I see beings
Like we ...with heads, arms, legs
Like we... I see them ..... I see them ......
My people, praising the coming
Some singing
Some dancing
Some swimming in the water for touch and see......

(As a people we have been waiting for a sign
Waiting for Makonaima to return, just like your Christ.
We have been waiting for ours.)... Some were fearful as
they stepped from baby boat to sandy shore.
"Surely," we said , "Our spirit God would look like us
Would dress like us?
Would talk like us?
Surely !!!"
Some stayed for a while. They were like medicine
men,Sorcerers with a black book in their hands and a
spirit wand they call a Cross. We know of this book. As
black is the colour of profound meaningful life, so this

33

book we know must contain power. At first, some people considered them cannibals, zombies, the children of dry bones, dai-dai with eyes like fire and the flesh stripped from their bodies so that the blood of their veins could be seen. They would parade with this cross-like thing, with the figure of a man, bleeding and dying, just like our head-hunters. They must be human-hunters. They talked of drinking his blood and the beauty of washing in its light.

That's when I had the Dream-Vision of darker skin people, Ancestral spirits coming, coming here to Arawak Country with people whose skin had been separated from their flesh. I saw trees, pulled up by their roots. I saw the river drying up and returning to the sky, my people infested, mother with child diseased, beautiful animals extinct. I saw the dark ones grow to love us like our ancestral brothers, skin like gold, dark purple, blue and mud-like red. I saw these other beings separating the land. I saw the land being pulled back and the womb of the earth sprawled apart. Gold, diamond, bauxite, wood. Just like their God, they separated the earth, the body, the heart and soul.

I awoke and told the elders at council about my vision, but they laughed hard as if my story was for children. And they said, "Who are you Haburi? It is said your wife was a frog. Ha!Ha!Ha!"
I broke my spear, threw my quiver and arrow into the fire.
I acted so they could see I meant ... no joke.
But they laughed with their presents of beads and looking-glass laughing back at them - they would not over-stand. Since then I have been shunned as if I had slept with my sister, because of my vision and their mis-vision.

That was then, a long, long, time ago - the year 1492, and we are now in the year 1992 and I have seen my vision like bad witch-craft come true. The name of that man, that pirate, that clown who had no longitude, that lascivious undiscovered European ....

34

whose......name...was...Chrisss...Christooooo...some..
thing.....
...Lubber..or..Lumber..or..Lumbus.
The last I heard about him was that he died in obscurity,
but that was a long, long, time ago!!
Like a Dream-Vision of many many different images
I see...some good...I see...some bad...
I see...some neither good or bad.

Only Makonaima and Orehu know.
Only Makonaima and Orehu know..

Signed: Haburi c/o Tuup Hell's Midden Kitchen

POUR QUI   POUR QUOI

POUR QUI   POUR QUOI
Arawaks Caraibes   Incas Mayas Aztèques
Peuples déracinés...............................
Merveilles de l'Altiplano   englouties
Oubliées...............   ....
Rumeurs de l'Orénoque   Ses brunes eaux
Douceâtres murmurent encore leurs noms
Cristobal Colon..............Encomienda......
POUR QUI   POUR QUOI
La croix épouse l'épée,........................
Ils se nomment désormais justiciers
Meurtres Pillages aux visages camouflés..........
Anacoana.......Higuanoma.......Suppliciées
AU NOM DE QUI   AU NOM DE QUOI
Tes cavaliers de l'apocalypse font irruption
Cupides sournois...............................
Raz de marée qui déferle et écume................
Il gronde "Le Christ et l'or ou la mort"
AU NOM DE QUI   AU NOM DE QUOI
Les fleurs du mal poussent sur l'arbre de la foi
Branches de crucifix et d'épées....................
Elles portent et donnent les fruits de..............
Fausses identitées   Mots passe-partout.............

35

Fourre-tout d'altérités...................
AU NOM DE QUI   AU NOM DE QUOI
Ton histoire est glorifiée dans les musées...................
Ton nom gravé en or sur les monuments aux morts ..
POUR QUI   POUR QUOI
Dans les cahiers des écoliers des pages blanches
Restent muettes......Le souvenir se tait indigne
Les livres d'histoire restent des cicatrices mal refermées
Mémoires de terres usurpées   De gloires falsifiées.........
POUR QUI   POUR QUOI
Héros ou martyres   Bourreaux ou victimes.....
Avec ou sans toi Cristobal Colon L'Europe continue
De s'approprier le Monde............................
Elle cherche éperdue le jardin d'Eden   Obscur paradis
inconnu
POUR QUI   POUR QUOI
Les Indes te narguent...................................
L'Amérique soigne encore ses blessures...................
Continents qui n'en finissent pas de mourir............
Fébrilement le soleil se lève sur une nouvelle humanité..
Timide et pâle comme une aurore boréale................

POUR TOUT CELA   POUR TOUS CEUX-LA
Le Présent a du mal à enfanter................
Un futur plus humain. Volcan endormi..........
Témoin il attend   Battements incessants dans les
Oubliettes du temps,.......................
Il reste inaccessiblement............
Suspendu dans l'espace.............

Allix Belrose-Huyghues

For Whom   For What

FOR WHOM   FOR WHAT
Arawaks Caribs Incas Mayas Aztecs
Uprooted peoples................
Marvels of Altiplano   swallowed up
Forgotten...........................
Rumours of the Orinoco   Its brown waters
Sweetly murmur still their names
Cristobal Colon.............. Encomienda....
FOR WHOM   FOR WHAT
Cross marries sword....................
They are called henceforth dispensers of justice
Murders   Ransackings with camouflaged faces
Anacoana .... Higuanoma......... Torture victims
IN THE NAME OF WHOM   IN THE NAME OF WHAT
Your horsemen of the apocalypse burst in
Deceitful rapers....................
Tidal wave which breaks and foams.........
It growls "Christ and gold or death"
IN THE NAME OF WHOM   IN THE NAME OF WHAT
Sick flowers grow on the tree of faith
Branches of crucifix and swords..............
They bear and give the fruits of
False identities   Passwords..............
Junk-room   of   othernesses................
IN THE NAME OF WHOM   IN THE NAME OF WHAT
Your history is glorified in museums..........
Your name engraved in gold on the monuments to the
dead....
FOR WHOM   FOR WHAT
Heroes or martyrs .... Executioners or victims
With or without you Cristobal Colon   Europe continues
To take over the world ....
Lost, she seeks the garden of Eden   Hidden unknown
paradise....
FOR WHOM   FOR WHAT
The Indies are taunting you.............................
America still nurses its wounds...................
Continents which are in the throes of death........
Feverishly the sun rises on a new mankind........
Timid and pale like an aurora borealis.....

FOR ALL THAT   FOR ALL THOSE
The present has difficulties giving birth........
A future more humane ...... Dormant volcano....
Witness, it waits   Incessant beatings in the
Secret cells of time ....
It remains inacessibly........
Suspended in space........

Allix Belrose-Huyghues

Tempest

Something like a prophetic blast
Like the gods raging in eternity
Speeds this green world in wonders of becoming;
A lightning shock shapes the living
Into memories of the heroic dead;
Thunder cracks, rain pours
The river of multiplying Calibans,
Islands peopled in the quest of the ancient mariner;
Hurricanes howl
Calling each generation by a magic name
And the angry volcano spurts a witchcraft
Of the language-sucking beast as the saviour of souls;
The wild winds breathe fire
As the broken empire falls in a landslide,
Then the earth opens with a grunt
Swallowing all unbelievers
In a sign of the slave's last hunt.

Faustin Charles

Aborigine

(For Derek Walcott)

History is a madman
Dreaming he is sane.
Blood vessels spout
Mahogany-rain and sun-ripen juice,
Raging, washing away the memory
Of homicidal philistines
And ancient fortresses.
Cannibal teeth lust in the vein,
Rip the heart, then fall silent
To the plume of rainbow feathers
Adjusted to the necromancy of the brain.
Civilization,
Uncompromising in its discontents,
Has destroyed the tree-top palaces,
The spontaneous jungle and life-giving volcano,
Leaving only the unconscious vision of language.

(Mind is greater than body, body must die,
But mind lives forever in the wind;
Mind moves matter, transforms colour and movement)

See, touch, taste the purifying imagery.

Faustin Charles

39

Seashells To Your Ear
(for Eddie Kamau Brathwaite)

Hold that seashell to your ear
tell me what you hear

columbus ships
lovers lips
sound of whips
footfalls on the plank
choose the tide
instead of chains
seagulls glide
in the mirror
of a terrible blue
land ahead
forget the dead
spirits of the deep
confide in drowned gourds
ancient things
beneath the seagull wings
carib shards leap
through seep of bone
crack of stone
black hollers
turning blue
echo arawak
in lap of coral
throat of seagull
fatal sabotage flight
in eye of flying fish
no survivors
cubana lamentation
in broad sunlight
honeymooning sharks
bellyful of trinkets
off devils island
swoon to muskets
arrowhead songs in seaweed
rocks that bleed
play of power
in a bay of pigs

lovers tongues
the hush of pebbles
seagulls forever wheeling
in a blue passage

Hold that seashell to your ear
you who dare the breath of history

Now offer a flower to the sea
Become a lover

risen from the ruins

John Agard

These Rocks

history maketh homage
to these rocks
where carib heels

        embraced an abyss

history maketh homage
to these rocks
where a god of wind

        engraved enigmas

history maketh homage
to these rocks
though they absent

        from history books

so passing stranger
to these rocks

        ponder where you place your feet

this island hold history
in these rocks

        which are the knuckles
        of forgotten gods

John Agard

Ode to Waitukubuli

Land where we were born
Where Arawaks and Caribs fought
The French and English too
A land where slaves labored

Their sweat...My blood
Their blood... My sweat
Their toil...Our homeland
Oh Waitukubuli
Your flora, fauna, water wonder,
Now rechristened Dominica.
Land of nature, bountiful and blessed
Oh oasis of Karifouna
Slaves to be sold and slave to sell
Old market, New Market
Old World, New World, Third World, Same World
The 365 rivers flow providing energy
The electricity of my brains,
Forging my liberty, creating my path
Securing my inheritance, my Waitukubuli
My Dominica, my homeland to love.
To cherish and to fight for.

Oh Waitukubuli
Sing so that your children will remain free
And that the Sisserou will continue to roost
In the mountain
High on tree tops.
Oh Waitukubuli my losses I forget,
My strength I regain
In my desire to fulfil a secure future for the children
Lest they die without knowing...
Blood is red, sweat is wet
Tears are natural.
Are all ingredients in becoming
One nation... one people
Existing in love and fellowship.

Let my blood be your tears,
My sweat your blood,

42

My nation our nation.
Together we will protect the Sisserous...
The Boiling Lake
Trafalgar
Together we will walk to the mountain land
for it refuses to come to us.
Give praise and thanks for Waitukubuli.
Lift up your heads
And smell the scent of the rivers flowing
And kiss the dream of you and I
Oh Waitukubuli! My homeland.

Harold Sealey

REVELATIONS

(I)

Arawidi, Arawidi

I've been watching the edge of the world
Edging in closer and closer....

Eating up every thing like termites
or like the burrow fly which lays its eggs
the brood eats up every thing with an
insatiable appetite.
The wind plays the sweet songs of
Amacaliva,
the sea gives way,
Mummer Oedu is dying
water mummer children don't sing no more
by light of moon,
mystifying the minds of sea-men.

Brother Arawidi weeps rays of light
which burn the brains of mad dogs and
English men who do not take mid-day
sleep, chew coco leaf or peyote,
give thanks in cloud smoke, weed of wisdom
corridors to alter-dimensional reality,
they do not sit on the belly of our
earth mother but bore into her flesh,
they do not do as we do.

They are at the edge of the world and
I've been watching the edge of the world
edging in ... closer ... and ... closer....

Pentagon hand shakes, the state declares,
that the people are the-e-e
enemy of the state,
the people's national army kills children
mothers weep for their husbands and the
American government is open for business
refugees, refugees, refugees.
Teaching farmers to kill
sowing seeds of bullets,
hungry bellies of lead cut down your harvest
Americans feast on death meat

and they like their meat ..... rawwWWW.
CIA.FBI.KKK, death squads and the slimy
hands of multi-mega-governmental-
inventions of war-toys, torture-control,
World Domination and the-e-e American way.
Guns, guns, guns for sale.
Border patrol
keeping people out,
keeping people in,
Mexico/Guatemala/Honduras/Nicaragua/
Costa-Rica/Panama/Caribbean-Native-
Amerindian-Arawak/El Salvador....
Midden's kitchen, back door Politics/
as phosphorus bombs land on mountains
children lose their families
and families lose themselves
torture, torture, torture,
the Aboriginal indigenous
human beings
the North American Indian
the South American Indian
the Central American Indian
the Amerindians from around the sea.
Detention Reservation for Refugees
Violates and is a Violation of Human
Rights and International Law.
Geneva Convention, do your fucking job
and stop the American government from
assassinating the world.

TV, radio, satellite, banker's card,
watching me watching it, watching it watching
me, watching the edge of the world edging
in closer and closer....

While I sat in my benab, hammock in swing, I
saw rocket ship leaving Mountain Ridge,
I saw the heavens open up, fire ball red
satellite rocket.
Guyana land mark sight.
But they are fools. Don't they know

that we are one of the first people to
have come from the sky,
Our Ancestors with skin like gold, dark
purple blue, and mud-like red?...
just like the Eagle
we will fly in the ether
and return
to the sky.....

Read a legend, drink a myth, taste of
reality ... D.N.A. last dream wish

Freedom, Liberty and Human Rights
Columbus howls like a jackal

Freedom, Liberty and Human Rights
Columbus howls like a jackal......

Signed: Haburi c/o Tuup   Hell's Midden Kitchen

On Christopher Colombus: View from the Crevice

We saw you
coming
Through our crevices of leaves

Blinding in armour
Stumbling in the surf
With your handful of wet-plumed plunderers.

Didn't you too have sons?
Diego and Ferdinand
Prince and Bastard who would write your name in history
Decades of sons who helped you decimate ours forever.

Blind stumbler
Wilful falcon
a fistful of surf on our beach.

Today they would sing you, hail conqueror
As new fascists emerge
Creating heroes out of sea-spray
Presenting more buccaneers to build new walls
Making commonwealths out of bloody hope
Forgetting long marches
The great leaps, ujaamas,
The changed winds

Creating heroes and markets out of sea-spray.

Who orchestrated the falls?
Did they begin from you?
Clawing up our sands, tearing down our mud walls and temples
Laying a commonweal of false foundations.

Who orchestrated the dominoes?
Falling so neatly,
In line
In time -

On line
On time -
Noisy musicians and bricklayers interfacing,
fiber-opticking,
coming in
on line
as planned
creating a mosaic, of new walls
of world order
of world power
an orchestrated symphony of new plunder.

We saw you - blind stumblers who welcomed you.
But do we see you now - any better
Today?

Who orchestrates the people
So Maurice can be killed
Walter blown to bits
Haiti a pit
Nkrumah tumbles, Tiananmen explodes
Biko is mangled, Che desecrated
Chernobyl just happens?

Who is orchestrating Nostradamus?
So Allende is gunned down, Jara chopped off
And Rajiv removed?
The councils emerge
Caesars federate
And the bears and the red, white and yellows
And Blues
Hold hands across the spray
Planning the decimations and drenchings of all the
crevices
Again.

The leaves tremble
And new caciques come now
Bearing gifts

They are all in the marketplaces, drunken Amerindians
Whitened sepulchres - silenced - reserved
Playing dominoes.

The people play mas'
Become looters and leaders
And Senderos cannot sing another last song.

The fetuses have been forcepped, mangled and crunched
Tumbling out as bloody pulp
And more widows are coming through our crevices of
leaves.

But the gods and goddesses doan sleep.
Sing Marrons, Sing ! SING MARRONS, SING !
Remember, remember, remember
Senderos and Senderitas
Haydee and Nanny
And Biko and Jara's last songs.

Marina Ama Omowale Maxwell

I Will Enter

Singed by a flight of scarlet ibises
blinded like a grasshopper by the rains

tattered and hungry
you took me in

gave me cassava bread
and casirri

a hammock to sleep in

a blanket woven by
your own hands
rich with embroidery

I will   enter into you
I will   enter into you
                woman

through the Indian forest
of your hair
I will enter

through the passage of your
wary watchful eyes
I will enter

through the bitterness
of your cassava touch
I will enter

and when you are moonsick
I will bleed with you

But wait
like a broken flute
your tongue is silent
your eyes speak of an
ancient weariness
I too have known
memory is written
in each crumpled fold
you can still remember
how they pitted gun against
arrow
steel against stillness

Stunned by their demands
for gold.

Grace Nichols

Vagrant Flower

Wide-eyed staring
Wide-eyed staring

at silver threads
of rain descending
she looks colourless now
with the blight
of mental illness

Wide-eyed staring
Wide-eyed staring

at virgin soil
staining streams
from her palms
ascending
she moves listless now
on memory's sodden ground

Feed her symbols
take her back
to sapodilla breasts
and flaming poincianas
where her passions grew
concealed

Feed her symbols
take her back
through slippery
hollows
and risen mounds
of ferns
the mating songs
of birds building
nests

Feed her symbols
take her back
let her linger
longer

Where her breath
was first taken
away

Virgin soil of the Blessed Virgin
Conceiving without sin -
prayer of her forebearers
pray then for her
children

Wide-eyed staring
Wide-eyed staring

For on this
plot of land
the first blood
stone of builders
did befall her
heavily

Wide-eyed staring
Wide-eyed staring.

Abdul Malik

Not Hands Like Mine

Not hands
like mine
these Carib altars knew:
nameless and quite forgotten are the gods;
and mute,
mute and alone,
their silent people spend
a ring of vacant days
not like more human years,
as aged and brown their rivers flow away.

Yes, pressing on my land,
there is an ocean's flood;
it is a muttering sea.

Here, right at my feet
my strangled city lies,
my father's city and my mother's heart:
hoarse, groaning tongues,
children without love,
mothers without blood
all cold as dust, nights dim, there is no rest.

Ah!
mine was a pattern woven by a slave
dull as a dream encompassed in a tomb.

Now still
are the fields
covered by the floods;
and those rivers roll
over altars gone;
naked, naked loins
throbbing deep with life
rich with birth indeed
rouse, turning to the sun.

And more fierce rain will come again tonight
new day must clean,
have floods not drowned the fields
killing my rice and stirring up my wrath?

Martin Carter

Weroon   Weroon

I came to a benab
sharpening my arrow of stone
knitting my hammock of air
tying my feathers all around my head.

Then I drank from the calabash of my ancestors
and danced my dance of fire
Weroon   Weroon.

And I prayed to the blue ocean of heaven
dreaming of the voyage of death
and my corial of paradise paddling forever.

Now I climb toward the hole of heaven
and my hands are stretched to the altar of God
O wonder of all the stars departed
Weroon   Weroon   Weroon...

Martin Carter

Through Arawak Eyes

Through Arawak eyes I've long watched
your high grey Northland cities
and the pale ones running in circles
as if the Sun was a story
that they have never been told - Through Arawak eyes
Through Arawak eyes...
Through Arawak eyes....

Through Arawak eyes I've watched
the southern morning breaking
over the wide Atlantic
in a silver northbound plane
where the scarlet sky knew nothing
of brown men down below dying
and wished Columbus had turned
his tall ships back forever
to the cursed shores of Spain -
Through Arawak eyes...
Through Arawak eyes....

Through Arawak eyes I learned
of life from a gentle man
brown from the touch of the sun
who walked the green forests of Guyana
like a king in his palace in the sun
where no anthems could ever stop him
and the world from being one -
Through Arawak eyes...
Through Arawak eyes...

Through Arawak eyes I've searched
for answers to why the gentle fall
before the black and bloodied boots
of the blind and deaf invaders
and wondered when the mad World
will at last find its cure
deep in the Amazon green
of my jungles and mountains -
Through Arawak eyes...
Through Arawak eyes....

Through Arawak eyes I've watched
Your alabaster body bend
like a silver dandelion
in the shifting summer wind
and knowing you too will soon
be blown away - I cannot blame you
for the sins of your fathers
as I hide you in my arms
away from the crooked wheel
they left you rolling on
long long ago....long long ago...
Through Arawak eyes...
Through Arawak eyes...
Through Arawak eyes....

David Campbell

I Have Survived

I have survived
the crucible you chained my fathers in,
and you ask me.......who am I?
who am I?
I am......
Geronimo, Atahualpa, Juarez and Sitting Bull Brown...
Martin Luther King, George Jackson, and Ghandi
Brown...
Demerara, Jamaica and Mississippi Brown...
Miscegenation, Napalm, and Starvation Brown...
Rape, Lynch and Slave Brown...
Maracas, Drum-beat, and Sun Dance Brown...
            Eternal tourist...You may hide your icy eyes
from the spinning of my red Blood and Sun Wheel...
        You may close your ears from the deep pulse
of our Mother the Earth, under your careless feet...
        You may christen me and mine with Coca-Cola,
to our North, South, East and West...
        And as the Muzak plays, you may wrap me
in my brother's shroud of rain-bow brown...
        BUT...
Out of the sea-bed of my search-years
I have put together again

59

a million fragments of my brothers' ancient mirror...
and as I look deep into it
I see a million shades of fractured brown,
merging into an unstoppable tide....

David Campbell

REVELATIONS

(II)

A Carib Question

When our world began
We all were One

When your world was "new"
You designed and drew

You waged your war
And created Four

Now the world is old
Through lust for gold

Do we still live as One
Under Our God the Sun?

Annie Jagdeo

Hatuey

De nite did'n have no moon an like even de stars did fuhget to come out ... an de whole house was quiet quiet quiet.... wuz two bedroom wid seven children in two big bed ... all seven ah we ranging from fourteen years old to five ... all seven ah we waitin waitin in de dark wid de window done shut tite an de mosquito net tuck in under de fibre mattress.

Granma come in siddong on de bed, prop up she pillow, settle she self an den call out,
"Aye Beti, Beta allyu sleeping?"
"Nooo Granma."
"Aye! ah thought so!"
Granma stand up, unknot she hair, an it just uncoil like ah big snake, slip dong she back an stop just pas she waist.
"Allyu ready ?"
"Yesss Granma."
"Crick!"
"Crack!"
"Monkey break he -"
"Back!"
"Fuh ah piece a pommeh -"
"Rac."

An story take off.

"Well on de farm wey yuh Granpa an me wuz livin it had ah ole ole man ... he wuzen Indian like we ... he wuzen African an he wuzen Carib nida ... but he did look like he did have lil bit lil bit ah all three ... Aye Beti, Beta allyu lissenin?"
"Yesss Granma!"
"Well is he wot tell mih dis story bout dis Carib chief who did gie de Spanish an dem alot alota trouble ... an dis Carib chief an he people use to live right here in dis village ... ahmmmm wot he did name again? doan tell mih ah fuget he name ... anyway it go come back to de ole brain jus now."

Granma sit back dong, light up ah cigarette, take ah long drag an start up again. An we lissening to how she voice sounin nuh - how it fullin up de room nuh an jus floatin wid de singing ah de insects an frog an ting coming in from outside - an we hearin bout dis Carib chief who tell de Spanish Governor an dem "No" - "No" he ent go work fuh dem - "No" he ent sendin none ah he people from he village under he rule to work fuh dem - "No" he ent care nutten bout de Spanish Governor, de Spanish Queen or de King nida.

"Yuh see Beti, Beta de Carib an dem coulda fight an dis chief wuz ah warrior, an some ah dem did radda dead dead fighting dan be slave - over in Grenada dey did dash dey self over ah precipice radder dan surrender to de French. Allyu listenin?"

"Yesss Granma."

Now we seein an hearin Granma like if we in ah dream ... now we **seein** de chief an de whole village wid dey bundle on dey back, an de small children runnin to keep up wid de big people ... we **seein** dem headin for de hills up in Santa Cruz ... we **seein** dem hidin behind tree, movin quiet quiet quiet, not even de little baby an dem cryin ... we **seein** de Spanish soldier an dem wonderin whey dey gorn, whey to look, cause de whole village just disappear when dey come fuh dem.
"Well de nex mornin wot yuh think happen?"
"Wot Granma?"
"Jumbie take dem - Dey fall dong ah precipice?!"
"Nah boy de Carib an dem di know every track in de mountain!! ent? Granma ent?"
"Aie Beta - is true - but de Spanish an dem was determine like de devil to capcha dem, so dey torcher people from ah next village to make dem track he dong. .... So de chief realize dey ent stand ah chance, cause dey did'n have guns like de Spanish .... so he make ah plan. He go make de Spanish follow he by leavin a trail for dem, but de whole village go take ah different track leaving no trail at all for ah next place miles away. Dat

was ah master plan eh Beti, Beta?"
"Yess Granma."

Well now we out dey too... Now we an de whole village movin one one, one one like ants thru de hills ... now we wid de chief, runnin an walkin, runnin an walkin for three days an three nites... how on de fourth day when he sure in he mind that he people reach this odder place an dey safe, dat he decide to walk back to meet de soldiers dat huntin he.

"Nooo Granma - he carn do dat!"
"He shoulda draw he gun an -"
"Hush na boy, yu think he wuz de Lone Ranger! Yu en hear Granma say de Carib did'n ha no gun."
"Yeh Beti, Beta, he did'n ha no gun but he walk back brave an strong cause he know he people safe an he know de Spanish Governor an dem woulda stop dey search when dey find he - so he walk proud, he walk wid he head touchin sun an moon same time."

Now we **seein** de chief han tie up an dey torcherin he to make he say whey all he people hiding... an we hearin de Governor sentence he to burn alive till he dead for disobeying he orders.... an we seeing dem who working fuh de Spanish Queen standing round looking sad an helpless when de hour reach fuh de chief to geh execute.

"Well Beti, Beta, de ole man say as de Governor gie de order to lite de fire, one of de Katolik preece run up to de Chief an tell he to repent, to say he sorry so that he soul could go to heaven, ... an yuh know wot - yuh know wot!! - is den de chief open he mout fuh de first time since dey did capcha he ... He ask de Preece if de Governor going to go to heaven when he dead ... an de preece say yes ... so de chief shout out loud loud fuh all de Carib to hear - that he de chief en want to go to no heaven - he en want to go nowhere near de Governor even when he dead - Well is den de Spanish thought he was de devil self, cause he talking in such a rage thru de smoke an fire closing in on he - cause he en even fraid de fire an he only calling for vengeance, so de Preece an dem start pelting he wid big stone an...."

Now we eye open big big so in de dark, an de bed sheet covering we pull up right up to here almost covering we whole face - cause we **feelin** de heat.

"Granma, Granma, stop stop, doan say no more!"
"Well allyu ready to sleep now eh? Ah tell yu - Crick!"
"Crack!"
"De wire bend an mih story end."
"Granma, Granma, whey de chief people en up - wot happen wid dem?"
"Well dem en up in Lopinot an de Spanish never find dem till dis day."
"Granma, Granma, ent de chief name wuz Hatuey, ent?"
"Look here allyu too dam brite fuh me yes! Dat wuz he name self - Hatuey - now hush allyu mout an sleep else I en comin back with no more story next month."
"Yesss Granma."

Well sametime ah owl s-c-r-e-e-c-h ... lord ... an de whole house just vibrate like ah doe know what .... so yu know who everybody think that wuz!!

Zena Ali Puddy

Hummingbird

As I see you now
boyhood memories
fill my mind:
you
poised projectile
with blurred wings in motion
perpetually probing...

Legendary memories
of you and Iere's god
taking his revenge in pitch
on native warriors
who wantonly slew you
come to me...
You, in forest areas
of Palo Seco/Erin
where time traveller Bulbrook
searched the earthen past
for stories of
your contemporary Arawaks
flit across my mind...

Now, darting among my flowers
pausing poised you probe
into your future.
Could you have seen
civilization's slingshots
aimed at you,
you would have migrated
to the Amazon basin
or some such haven
to live in your pristine splendour;
but like the Amerindians
you could not withstand
the clash of culture.

And now, you pause here
and I recall...
But yesterday
you
were a totem in the land
and today
a living museum piece

Anson Gonzalez

68

Sales Drop

Not so?! ah say so
Not so?! ah say so

Well dey label de Arawak
    timid
an dey label de Carib
    fierce
Babylon system am-bush dem
Babylon system a-crush dem
Babylon system a-hush dem
Babylon system a-claim dem
Babylon system a-shame dem
For
  Five
    Hundred
      Years

Not so?! ah say so
Not so?! ah say so

Well dey seal up de Arawak
    image
an dey seal up dey Carib
    jeers
Babylon system a-mark dem
Babylon system a-chart dem
Babylon system a-plot dem
Babylon system a-hatch dem
Babylon system a-brew dem
For
  Five
    Hundred
      Years

Not so?! ah say so
Not so?! ah say so
Well dey labelling **Arawak**
    chickens
an dey labelling **Carib**
    beers

Babylon system a-sell dem
Babylon system a-buy dem
Babylon system a-eat dem
Babylon system a-drink dem
Babylon system a-waste dem
For
   Five
      Hundred
         Years

Not so?! ah say so
Not so?! ah say so

So leh we seal off dis Arawak
     dealing
an seal off Carib
     shares
Cause
Babylon system ab-duct dem
Babylon system a-mock dem
Babylon system a-wuck dem
Babylon system a-ting dem
Babylon system a-jinx dem
For
   Five
      Hundred
         Years

Not so?! ah say so
Not so?! ah say so

Abdul Malik

Arawak Chicken and **Carib Beer** are brand names in Trinidad.

Columbus And Me

Anytime I have to fly anywhere
on a plane
I does always find out
if the pilot is left-handed

The whole thing goes back
to the year 1934
I was seven years old
in Class One
Of the Anglican Primary School
in St. Vincent, British West Indies

There was 35 of us in the class
boys and girls

Can you imagine anything more boring
than sitting with 34 other people
ALL seven years old!!!

Our teacher, Miss Rodrigues,
was very, very old ——-
We figured her for about 17 or 18.......

One morning in history class
She told us
that Columbus
figured he could reach the East
by sailing West !!!

We all loved Miss Rodrigues
But we concluded she had to be crazy
Nobody in his right mind
would try to reach the East
by sailing West
After all
200 years before Columbus
Marco Polo had done
a very honest thing :-
He reached China
by walking East - WALKING East ....

71

So, Brother Columbus,
How lazy can you get !!!

Miss Rodrigues saw the doubt
                in our eyes
So she went and brought a globe....
And she spin the globe
from left to right -
West to East -
the way they say the earth does turn....

That is when we realize
she was left-handed -
Furthermore
Columbus had to be left-handed,
Because any honest god-fearing person
Bound to spin a globe from right to left.....

About 12 years later
Miss Rodrigues and I
had a brief affair
And one night
when I was tall and strong
and fully standing
she whispered to me
"How did you find out
            I am left handed?"

So I told her what she wanted to hear,
    I told her -
"It was the day
in 1934
when you and Columbus
                talk to me."

Shake Keane

Quinquennial

Near 500 years
since visionbungler Cristoforo
stumbled
on our paleolithic shores

Near 500 years
of slow torture

endured of majestic europeans
500 years milked dry
and bones left to parch
in the desert of economic
frustration

Near 50 irksome years
of striving

for responsibility
with paths marked by a few
who refused to let
hoodwinking europeans
stamp upon
our inborn desire
for nationhood

Near 50 years while
the intellectual plasma

grew and multiplied
into gigantic organism
pulsating threatening
till

Five years ago
with timidity

the europeans
in danger of exclusion
by their peers
fearful of consequences
of temerarious refusal
of our just demands
returned our country
to its people

Five plodding years
attempting the remaking

of slave into citizen
five years inching along
the timeless road of progress
five cataclysmic years
in our thinking
the world marvels
at our unruffled success

Anson Gonzalez

73

Bamboo Talks

bamboo talks
listen to it
- it knows our history
it saw all who colonized us
from the first who claimed
to have found us
when they really invaded us

bamboo talks
listen to it
it knows our history
- shed a tear
for every Amerindian man
beaten and tricked
for every woman raped
- there are no more tears left
that accounts for its hollowness

bamboo talks
for those who have ears
inward ears to listen
- listen
it is saying
'I do not like what I see'
it is saying
'The cycle of exploitation
is repeating itself'

bamboo talks
listen to it
because good historians
never die
never re-arrange facts
to hide the truth
- listen
it is saying
'Brother don't be fooled
keep your head to the sun'

bamboo talks
it knows exploiters
never listen
it is speaking
to you brother/sister
it is tired of seeing you bow
it is saying
'Keep your head to the sun'

Paula Obe Thomas

Imperial Illusion

Lie
under the imperial canopy
existing in a fanciful world
others envy your happiness

Tremors
shake you with a painful force
threatening to rip your entire being
into worthless, forgotten, fragments

Sapped
as the strain of physical solitude
oozes life from a limp body,
but the spirit lives.

Carlene Hall

Aspiration of a Ghetto Child.

Child of a minute
born of poverty and lust
doomed to a life of oppression
cursed from ancient times, black ghetto child.

The horrid cycle of life and death
senselessly broadcast to the innocent
stamps hatred in the hearts of another generation
violence and survival become the cry.

Try ghetto child
let the raging fires of discontent
motivate you to aim for better
feel the cycle weaken, because you made
a different, difference.

Carlene Hall

Gold-Rush

500 years later
standing on the harbour of my consciousness
beneath
layers
and layers
pomp
circumstance
stripped
bedlam within me
rages unfettered
within this circus
this farce of a celebration

floating balloons
helium-filled rainbow dreams
festive bouquets
reinvent
the exploitation

amidst faces stretched wide
parodies of bliss
dancing
in the orgy
of commemorative glee
I stand

Who will stretch minds far
far back
to ancestors
raped
transplanted
uprooted
dispossessed
mailed by 4th class postage
to Spain
crushed under the black boot
of cultural and
economic imperialism?
standing here
500 years after fact

beneath the banners
the flags
enrobed in this farce
Suddenly!
five hundred years of smouldering
rage
erupts
boiling cauldron of anger
spills over on a hot, scorching day
"Columbus was a damn, blasted liar!"
while they stare
I walk away bitter
alone
for one brief moment
I make MY history
I make MY peace

Dawn Mahailia Riley

It Is Time

It is high time
whatever decrepit minds
may choose
to erect
another monument
to slavery, theft, corruption,
yes, let another idiot
create Columbus in stone
so shall he remain
cold, frozen
not to enjoy a moment of the land
whose people sleep in shacks
while billions waste on stone
to blind a tourist's eyes
yes, it is fitting
only cold
only no feeling
no heart
could be a proper setting
for one who chose to rob
our treasures
to win the heart of a Spanish Queen
only one of feelings so inferior
could visit bloodshed on the islands' scenes
Today
we slaughter him
without blood
make stone monument his eternal coffin
Today
we restore our gems
our stolen spirits
our music
our heroes
our smiles
all that was taken
Today we hang the Queen of Spain
and bring our children home
our warmth shall be ours forever
    No more
    No more

Come again in any disguise
and we shall rip aside your mask
and make cold stones your eyes.
To the idiot
a million Santa Domingan peasants
will decide.

Jean Binta Breeze

Glossary

Aiomon Kondi: the chief dweller-on-high of the Arawaks.
Allende: Chilean elected head of state assassinated in office.
Altiplano: a high plateau between Peru and Bolivia.
Amacaliva: Amerindian word for Sun God.
Amadlozi Amazulu: Zulu words meaning power to the sky.
Anacaona: was the Arawak wife of a Carib chief. She was hanged by the Spaniards.
Arawaks: commonly regarded as the first Caribbean peoples. They were a peace loving people.
Arawidi: Amerindian God.
Asgard: in Norse mythology Odin`s home.
Babylon System: Rasta term for Western "civilization".
Batos: a ball game.
Bauxite: raw material for the making of aluminium.
Bay of Pigs: failed C.I.A. invasion of Cuba.
Benab: Arawak house.
Beti, Beta: affectionate Hindi words meaning girl and boy.
Biko: Steve Biko - South African political activist murdered in police custody.
Bisiri: Amerindian wise person or teacher.
Boiling Lake: a sulphur lake.
Caciques: Arawak word for chief.
Casirri: Amerindian drink.
Che: Che Guevara - Argentinian-born hero of the Cuban Revolution.
Chernobyl: site of nuclear disaster in the Ukraine.
Colon: another name for Colombus.
Corial: a type of canoe.
Crick! Crack! etc...: traditional opening used by story tellers in the Caribbean.
Cristoforo: Christopher - Columbus`s name.
Dai-Dai: an ancient Amerindian being.
Devils Island: French penal colony.
Erin: a place in Trinidad.
Haburi: Amerindian explorer.
Iere: an ancient Amerindian name for Trinidad.

Iocuhuuague Maorocon: is the Supreme Being of the Arawaks, represented in a three-sided figure with a head, and known as "The One with a Mother but without a Grandfather".

Jara: Victor Jara - Chilean popular poet and musician tortured and murdered by the military.

Jumbie: Caribbean word for ghost.

Kamonatu: Amerindian God.

Karifouna: Carib name for a festival.

Makonaima: Amerindian God.

Marrons: (Maroons) - escaped slaves who organised to fight the European settlers.

Maurice: Maurice Bishop (1944 - 1983) - assassinated Prime Minister of Grenada.

Mummer Oedu: Amerindian Goddess of the Sea.

Nanny: Maroon military tactitian and chieftainess; National Heroine of Jamaica.

Nkrumah: Kwame Nkrumah (1909 - 1972) - first Prime Minister of Ghana.

Nostradamus: prophet who lived in France during sixteenth century.

Orehu: Amerindian Mother of the Sea.

Orinoco: a large river running through Venezuela.

Palo Seco: a place in Trinidad.

Play `mas: Trinidadian expression meaning to act in a carefree manner.

Rajiv: Rajiv Gandhi - Indian prime minister assassinated in office.

Senderos & Senderitas: Peruvian revolutionaries.

Shaman: a holy person with the gifts of healing and prophecy.

Sisserou: a species of parrot - the national symbol of Dominica.

Taino: sometimes used as another name for Arawak.

Tamosikabotano: an Amerindian god.

Tiananmen: square in Beijing where student protesters were killed.

Tiano: Arawak word meaning "peace".

Trafalgar: site of famous waterfall in Dominica.

Ujaamas: Swahili word meaning coming together of people for the common good.

Waitukubuli: original name for Dominica.

Walter: Walter Rodney - Guyana-born activist, murdered in Guyana 1980.

Woilbaka: Amerindian name for a canoe made from the mora tree.

Xamaca or Xaymaca: Arawak name for Jamaica.

Biographical Notes

John Agard was born and brought up in Guyana. He writes for both children and adults and is widely published. He performs his poetry around Britain and abroad and has had several television appearances. Publications include **Mangoes and Bullets** and **Say It Again Granny!**.

Allix Belrose-Huyghues is of parents from the "French speaking" Caribbean. She has spent a lot of her life in France but now lives and works in Germany. Her poetry has been published in several journals and anthologies including Panrun Collective's **De Homeplace**.

James Berry was born and brought up in Jamaica and now lives in Britain. He is much published, writing both for children and adults. He has been awarded several prizes including the National Poetry Prize in 1981 and the Smarties Prize in 1987. He was awarded the OBE for services to literature.

Jean Binta Breeze is from Jamaica. She currently lives and works in Britain. She is an accomplished poet and performer. She has several publications and recordings to her name. She performs to audiences throughout the world. Publications include **Riddym Ravings and Other Poems**.

David Campbell was born and raised in Guyana. His father was Arawak Indian and his mother was Guyana Portuguese. He now resides in Canada. He is a song writer with many albums to his name.

Martin Carter was born and educated in Guyana. He has been very active in politics (holding a ministerial post), in the academic world, as a historian and as a writer. Publications include **Poems of Resistance** and **Poems of Succession**.

Faustin Charles was born in Trinidad and now lives in London. He writes poetry, novels and short stories. He has edited several collections of folktales and short stories for young people. He has held several writers' residencies. He reads his poetry and tells stories to audiences all over Britain.

Mike Cleary: Londoner and lecturer. Member of Panrun Collective.

Anson Gonzalez publishes **The New Voices** and **The New Voices Newsletter** in Trinidad. A well-known poet, his collections include **Lovesong of Boysie b. and Other Poems,** and **Moksha: Poem of Light and Sound**. He has written many non-fiction works including several publications for children.

Carlene Hall lives in Trinidad and has previously had work published in **New Voices** and **De Homeplace**, Panrun Collective's collection of poems by young writers of Caribbean origin.

Annie Jagdeo is of Trinidadian/Carib descent, currently living in London.

Shake Keane was born in 1927 in St. Vincent. He has worked as a teacher, poetry reader, reporter, producer and jazz musician. He is much published and won the **Casa de las Americas** prize. He currently resides in New York.

Abdul Malik (Delano Abdul Malik De Coteau) founder member of, Panrun Collective, Malik now lives in Brixton but originates from Grenada and Trinidad. He spends much of his time working in education with adults and children, giving poetry performances and running workshops. Previous publications include **Black Up** 1972, **Revo** 1975, **The Whirlwind** 1988. Malik also composes music and has released two recordings of his poetry and music **More Power** 1981 and **More DAMD Power** 1986.

Marina Ama Omowale Maxwell is currently based in the U.S.A. but comes from Trinidad and Tobago. She has worked as a lecturer and video producer in the U.S.A., Europe and the Caribbean. Her publications include **The Weakened Sex** and **Chopstix in Mauby**.

Pamela C. Mordecai was born in Jamaica and educated in both the U.S.A. and the Caribbean. She has been a teacher, teacher trainer and has worked extensively in the media. She currently works at the University of the West Indies in Jamaica.

Grace Nichols was born in Guyana but now lives in Britain. She has written a novel, several poetry books, children's books and has edited anthologies. In 1983 she won the Commonwealth Poetry Prize. She performs her poetry in

Britain and abroad. Publications include **i is a long memoried woman** and **Whole of a Morning Sky.**

Zena Ali Puddy comes from Trinidad but spent several years living and working in education in Britain. She was very active in the promotion of Caribbean literature both as a lecturer and as a performer in the Jarai Theatre Company. She is currently living in Tobago. She is a founder member of Panrun Collective.

Dawn Mahailia Riley is currently based in the U.S.A. but comes from Trinidad. Her poems have been published in **The New Voices** and **De Homeplace**, (Panrun Collective).

Paula Obe Thomas comes from Trinidad. She has had her poems published in **The New Voices, Working Women News Letter** and various anthologies. She is also involved in popular education and music.

Harold Sealey comes from Dominica. He is a poet and dramatist and member of the Dominica Writers' Guild. He also writes short- stories for children.

Tuup (Godfrey Duncan). His poetry, stories and expressive/ experimental music are steeped in the oral traditions of Guyana originating from both the Amerindian cultures and West Africa. Both adults and children find him a spellbinding performer.

Hymie Wilson is originally from Jamaica. He has been living in England for many years. A prolific writer of tales and children's stories.

The editor and publisher would like to thank those writers whose poems and short stories appear here for the first time.

Specific credits: **Seashell To Your Ear; These Rocks** by kind permission of John Agard c/o Caroline Sheldon Literary Agency (c)1992. **Old Indian Remembering** reproduced with permission of Curtis Brown Group Ltd. London on behalf of Grace Nichols Copyright (c) Grace Nichols 1992.

Acknowledgements are also due to the editors and publishers of the following books and periodicals in which some of the contributions first appeared:

The Expatriate - Brookside Press Imprint (Arawak Adventurer, Tempest, Aborigine - Faustin Charles); **The Whirlwind** - Panrun Collective (Vagrant Flower - Abdul Malik); **i is a long memoried woman** - Karnak House 1983 (I will enter - Grace Nichols); **Savacou 7/8** (Nation Shout - Shake Keane); **COIP INDIGI & SA KA FET** (Ode to Waitubuli-Harold Sealey); **Poems of Succession** - New Beacon (Not Hands Like Mine, Weroon Weroon - Martin Carter).

Every effort has been made to trace copyright holders. Please contact us if you have not been acknowledged.